© Copyright 2018 by Yehudis Litvak

All rights reserved. This book or parts thereof may not be reproduced in any form, stored in any retrieval system, or transmitted in any form by any means—electronic, mechanical, photocopy, recording, or otherwise—without prior written permission of the publisher, except as provided by United States of America copyright law.

ISBN-13: 978-1725140165
ISBN-10: 1725140160

Cover design: Avigail Litvak

Ani Ve-Ami Jewish Living Education
http://ani-ve-ami.com/
aniveami@gmail.com

Ani Ve-Ami Curriculum Guide: Tanach

by Yehudis Litvak

Table of Contents

Foreword 5
Month 1 9
    Overview 9
    Materials 12
    Week 1 16
    Week 2 17
    Week 3 18
Month 2 19
    Overview 19
    Materials 21
    Week 1 24
    Week 2 25
    Week 3 26
Month 3 27
    Overview 27
    Week 1 32
    Week 2 33
    Week 3 34
    Week 4 35
Month 4 36
    Overview 36
    Materials 38
    Week 1 41
    Week 2 42
    Week 3 43
    Week 4 44
Month 5 45
    Overview 45
    Materials 47
    Week 1 50
    Week 2 51
    Week 3 52
    Week 4 53
Month 6 54
    Overview 54
    Materials 57
    Week 1 60
    Week 2 62

  Week 3 63
  Week 4 64
Month 7 65
  Overview 65
  Materials 68
  Week 1 71
  Week 2 72
  Week 3 73
Month 8 74
  Overview 74
  Materials 76
  Week 1 79
  Week 2 80
  Week 3 81
Month 9 82
  Overview 82
  Materials 84
  Week 1 87
  Week 2 88
  Week 3 89
  Week 4 90
Month 10 91
  Overview 91
  Materials 93
  Week 1 96
  Week 2 97
  Week 3 98
Appendix A: The 24 Books of the Tanach 99
Appendix B 101
  Required reading 101
  Books for additional reading 103
  Recommended music 104
  Recommended art 105
  Recommended poetry 106
  Map list 107

Foreword

Welcome to the Ani Ve-Ami Curriculum! This guide will help you navigate the curriculum and customize it to best fit your family's needs.

This guide covers:
- Tanach
- Jewish history
- Jewish literature
- Grammar
- Jewish music
- Jewish art
- Jewish poetry
- Geography

Additional materials needed:
- notebook (for each child)
- drawing paper
- pens, pencils, crayons

The books for required and additional reading, as well as recommended art, music, and poetry are listed in Appendix A.

To complete the curriculum, you will need:
- Ani Ve-Ami Jewish Year Curriculum Guide
- Weekly Parsha book(s) of your choice (see ani-ve-ami.com for recommendations)

- *The Story of the World* Volume 1 (this time period is covered in chapters 1 - 24; you can skip chapters 6 and 14, since this material is covered in Jewish history) and its accompanying Activity Book OR *The History of the Ancient World* Volume 1 (this time period covers parts 1 - 4) and its accompanying Study Guide; books listed on the ani-ve-ami.com website on the page for this time period (you may be able to borrow these books from your local library)

- a math curriculum of your choice (see ani-ve-ami.com for recommendations)

- a science curriculum of your choice (see ani-ve-ami.com for recommendations)

- a Hebrew language curriculum of your choice, as well as textual study resources, if desired (see ani-ve-ami.com for recommendations)

This guide breaks up the school year into ten month-long units. While most homeschoolers will begin using this curriculum in September, some families might structure their school year differently, or begin Ani Ve-Ami mid-year. For this reason, the months are numbered, but not named. It is up to each family to decide how the monthly breakdown corresponds to their own schedule.

In addition, some families may choose to go through the curriculum at a quicker pace, while others may find it more effective to slow down and spend more than a month on each unit. Perhaps your children are especially interested in a specific unit, or perhaps, you have a child with special needs who takes longer to absorb the material, or perhaps your family loves to travel or is otherwise too busy to fit everything in this guide into a tight schedule. That's perfectly fine. There is no right or wrong way to do this. This curriculum is meant to be adjusted to your family's unique needs.

This guide is intended for the whole family. The guidelines below describe how to use it for multiple children of different ages. Each child will be working on their own level, while at the same time participating in relevant family activities.

For each monthly unit, this guide offers a brief summary, as well as recommended reading and, sometimes, additional reading. The additional reading will sometimes take longer and overlap with the next monthly unit. Don't worry — some months don't have additional reading, and you won't fall behind.

If your children are young, you might want to omit the additional reading. If you have both older and younger children, you might use the recommended reading as a read aloud for the whole family and the additional reading as independent reading for your older children. If all your children are older, you can use both recommended and additional reading as read alouds, or you might assign some of either recommended or additional reading to your children to read independently. Feel free to experiment and see what works best for your family.

The monthly units also introduce your children to Jewish or Biblical-themed art, music, and poetry, with selections for each month that are relevant to the time period, either in content or because it was produced in that time period.

Each monthly unit contains three or four weekly units. Each weekly unit is based on a short story or book excerpt set in the times of the Tanach or a passage from the Tanach itself. In the beginning of the week, you can read the story or passage aloud to your children. In the following days, each of your children will do narration and copy work or dictation on the story or passage.

Depending on the age of the child, narration could be oral, pictorial, or written. For more on narration, see the How It Works section of the Ani Ve-Ami website.

Each weekly unit contains a paragraph for copy work or dictation and a grammar exercise based on that paragraph. A younger child should only copy a sentence or two. An older child should copy the whole paragraph and do the grammar exercise that accompanies it. For more on copy work and dictation, see the How It Works section of the Ani Ve-Ami website.

The monthly units also contain maps and directions for map work. We recommend that you make a copy of the map for each of your children and let them do the map work on their own level, with your help if necessary.

Month 1

Overview

This is the first month of the homeschooling year. If you are beginning your year in the fall, you will be busy getting ready for the Jewish holidays of the month of *Tishrei* (see our *Jewish Year Curriculum Guide* for more details).

Even if you begin your year in a different month, it might take you time to get into a routine, or you might want to review what you covered in the previous year. Therefore, for this month, we prepared only three weeks of learning. As always, if you find yourself with extra time, please see our recommendations for additional reading.

Focus of the month: בראשית - The book of *Bereishis* (Genesis)
Events: birth of Avraham - death of Yosef

Time period: years 1948 - 2309 on the Jewish calendar (years 1813 - 1452 BCE)

Brief summary of the time period:

In Ur Kasdim, Mesopotamia, a man named Avraham discovers G-d and renounces the idol worship practiced in those days. At G-d's command, he takes his family and travels to the land of Canaan, where he settles.

After many years of praying for children, Avraham's wife Sarah gives birth to a son, whom they name Yitzchak. Yitzchak continues worshiping one G-d, just like his father. He marries Rivka, his cousin, and they eventually have twin sons, Yaakov and Eisav.

Yaakov grows up to be a scholar, while Eisav becomes a hunter. Upon Rivka's advice, Yaakov tricks Yitzchak into giving him the blessing he'd meant for Eisav. Afraid of Eisav's wrath, Yaakov escapes to Charan, where he marries his cousins Leah and Rachel, as well as their servants, Bilha and Zilpa. Yaakov has eleven sons and a daughter, Dina. His favorite wife, Rachel, only bears one child, Yosef.

With his large family, Yaakov returns to the Land of Canaan and makes peace with Eisav. Rachel dies as she gives birth to Yaakov's twelfth son, Binyamin.

Yaakov is especially fond of Yosef. He gifts him with a special garment. The other brothers grow jealous of Yosef. They sell him into slavery. Yosef is taken to Egypt. Through a chain of events, he eventually becomes the ruler of Egypt, second only to Pharaoh himself.

A severe famine hits the land of Canaan, and Yaakov's sons are forced to travel to Egypt in order to buy food. Yosef recognizes them and tests their loyalty to their father and to Binyamin, his youngest brother. Eventually, he reveals his identity and invites his family to move to Egypt so that he could provide them with food in times of famine.

Yaakov's whole family moves to Egypt, to the land of Goshen. Due to Yosef's powerful position in Egypt, Yaakov's family lives in comfort. Yaakov grows old and dies. Later, Yosef dies.

Brief overview of books of the Tanach that are the focus of this month:

-- בראשית

Bereishis (Genesis) is the first of the books in the Tanach, and part of the Torah. It tells the story of the beginnings of the Jewish people, starting from the creation of the world and continuing with the forefathers and foremothers, the sale of Yosef, and Yaakov's family's descent to Egypt.

Materials

Recommended reading for this month:
Little Midrash Says Bereishis or *A Treasury of Torah Aggados*, volumes 1 and 2

Weekly reading:
Week 1: *The Prisoner*, from the book *The Prisoner and Other Tales of Faith* by Rabbi Salomon Alter Halpern
Week 2: *We Attack at Midnight*, from the book *The Prisoner and Other Tales of Faith* by Rabbi Salomon Alter Halpern
Week 3: *Bereishis*/Genesis 43:15 – 44:17

Grammar: *Grammar Land* by M. L. Nesbitt
Chapters 1: Judge Grammar and His Subjects; and 2: Mr. Noun

Geography:
Map #1. Charan, Canaan, and Ur Kasdim

Map work: trace Avraham's journey from Ur Kasdim, through Charan, to the Land of Canaan

Map #2. Canaan and Egypt

Map work: trace Yaakov's family's journey from Canaan to Egypt

Music: *I Made this World for You* by Rabbi Mordechai Dubin

Art: Yoram Raanan's Biblical art: https://www.yoramraanan.com/biblical-prints/

Poetry: Shabbat Hayom L'hashem (original Hebrew text and English translation available at http://www.zemirotdatabase.org/view_song.php?id=90)

Map #1. Charan, Canaan, and Ur Kasdim

Map #2. Egypt and Canaan

Week 1

From: *The Prisoner*, from the book *The Prisoner and Other Tales of Faith* by Rabbi Salomon Alter Halpern

Copy work/dictation passage:

Two guards led forward a boy of fourteen. His wrists were bound, and he wore prisoner's garb; but from his large dark eyes flashed such earnestness and purpose, so fearlessly did he carry his head, and such calm and resolution were expressed in the handsome young face framed in black locks, that exclamations of admiration escaped some of the onlookers.

Pay attention to punctuation.

Week 2

From: *We Attack at Midnight*, from the book *The Prisoner and Other Tales of Faith* by Rabbi Salomon Alter Halpern

Copy work/dictation passage:

Their progress was slow. The freed captives, mostly women and children, were unable to march quickly. Behind them came a long train of donkeys and camels laden with the recovered loot, or carrying those who were too weak to walk. At the head of the caravan rode Abram with his rescued nephew.

Underline all nouns.

Week 3
>From: *Bereishis*/Genesis 43:15 – 44:17
>Copy work: 43:15-18

You can copy the text from a *chumash* (or from sefaria.org) in the original Hebrew.
If you prefer English, here is a translation:

And the men took that gift, and double the amount of money in their hand, and Binyamin, and they rose and went down to Egypt, and they stood before Yosef. And Yosef saw them with Binyamin, and he said to the man in charge of his house, "Bring the men into the house and slaughter and prepare meat, because these men will eat with me at noon." And the man did as Yosef said, and the man brought the men to Yosef's house.

>Circle proper nouns.

Month 2

Overview

As families are still adjusting to this curriculum, and perhaps catching up from the Tishrei holidays, this month only contains three weeks of work. As usual, if you find yourself with extra time, please use the additional recommended reading, or focus on another subject that your children are particularly interested in.

Focus of the month: The books of שמות - *Shemos* (Exodus) and ויקרא - *Vayikra* (Leviticus)

Events: Yaakov's family's descent to Egypt - completion of the Mishkan (Tabernacle)

Time period: years 2309 - 2449 on the Jewish calendar (years 1452 - 1312 BCE)

Brief summary of the time period:

Yaakov and his family, numbering seventy people, descend to Egypt and settle in the land of Goshen. At first, they live in peace and partake of the bounty of the land. They have many children, and the Jewish population in Egypt grows quickly. The Egyptians begin to worry that their Jewish neighbors might turn against them, especially if there is a war. Pharaoh comes up with a cruel plan — enslavement.

Gullible Jews fall for Egyptian tricks, and soon most of them become slaves to the Egyptians, with the exception of the tribe of Levi. The Egyptians oppress the Jews and cause them tremendous suffering.

Two centuries after their move to Egypt, a new leader, Moshe, receives a command from G-d to take the Jews out of Egypt. After ten devastating plagues, the Jewish people leave Egypt and head to the desert, to worship G-d.

Forty-nine days later the Jews receive the Torah at Mt. Sinai, but only forty days after that the Jews build a golden calf. Moshe prays for the Jews, and G-d forgives them. They build a portable temple, called Mishkan, which they carry with them as they travel through the desert.

Brief overview of books of the Tanach that are the focus of this month:

שמות -

Shemos (Exodus) - second book of the Tanach, and second book of the Torah; covers Yaakov's family's descent to Egypt through the construction of the Mishkan

ויקרא -

Vayikra (Leviticus) - third book of the Tanach, and third book of the Torah; covers the laws of sacrifices in the Mishkan, as well as ritual purity

Materials

Recommended reading for this month:
Little Midrash Says Shemos and *Little Midrash Says Vayikra* or *A Treasury of Torah Aggados*, volumes 3 (all) and 4 (chapters 34 and 35)

Additional reading:
Elementary:
Shpeter by Rabbi Meir Uri Gottesman
My Last Year in Mitzrayim by Chaim Greenbaum
Middle grades:
Dual Discovery by Zecharia Hoffman

Weekly reading:
Week 1: *The Boy in the Basket*, from the book *The Prisoner and Other Tales of Faith* by Rabbi Salomon Alter Halpern
Week 2: *He Went Home*, from the book *The Prisoner and Other Tales of Faith* by Rabbi Salomon Alter Halpern

Week 3: Vayikra/Leviticus 19:1-18

Grammar: *Grammar Land* by M. L. Nesbitt
Chapters 3: Little Article; and 4: Mr. Pronoun

Geography:
Map #3. Egypt and the Sinai desert
Map work:
- trace the Jewish people's journey from Egypt to the desert
- make an educated guess where Mt. Sinai was

Music: *Let My People Go* by Rabbi Mordechai Dubin
Art: Ellen Miller Braun's microcalligraphy Hebrew art: https://ellenmillerbraun.com/the-book-of-exodus-the-parting-of-the-red-sea
Poetry: Song of the Sea in Shemos/Exodus 15:1-19

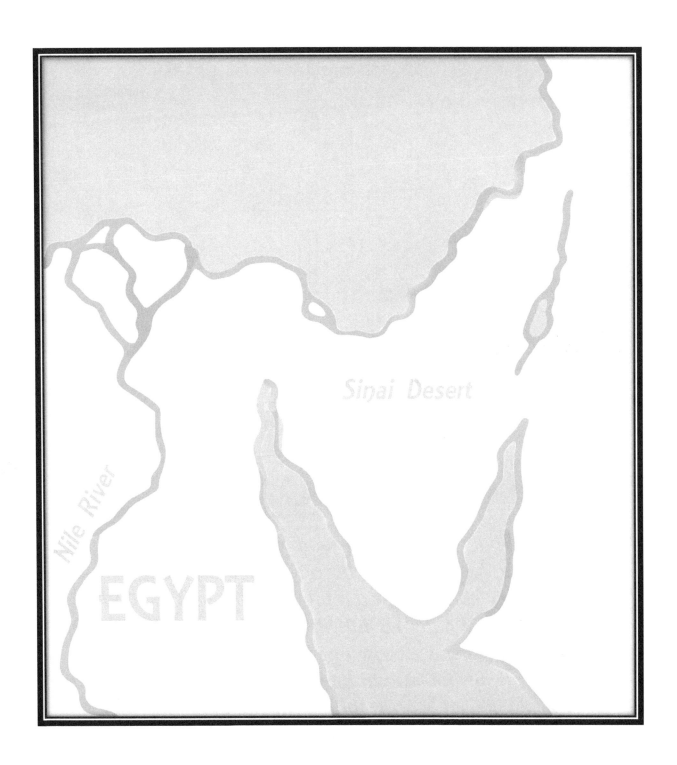

Map #3. Egypt and the Sinai Desert

Week 1

From: *The Boy in the Basket*, from the book *The Prisoner and Other Tales of Faith* by Rabbi Salomon Alter Halpern

Copy work/dictation passage:

She loved the baby. He was so good and so clever. They had to hide him, of course, for the Egyptians often came to see if any babies had been born. They had hollowed a niche in the wall, behind the bed-curtains, and there baby Toviah slept. He never cried, as if he understood how dangerous it was; of course he had no need to cry, for Miryam was always looking in to see if he was awake, and if she saw by the way he moved his lips that he was hungry, she took him straight to her mother.

Pay attention to punctuation. Underline all articles.

Week 2

From: *He Went Home*, from the book *The Prisoner and Other Tales of Faith* by Rabbi Salomon Alter Halpern

Copy work/dictation passage:

The gilt chariot with its well greased, leather-tyred wheels, ran smoothly on the paved road. He let the thoroughbreds run as fast as they pleased. The air rushed past him, and he felt the exhilaration of speed, but it could not make him forget the seriousness of his quest.

Pay attention to punctuation. Underline all nouns and circle all pronouns.

Week 3

    From: Vayikra/Leviticus 19:1-18
    Copy work: Vayikra/Leviticus 19:15-18

You can copy the text from a *chumash* (or from sefaria.org) in the original Hebrew.

If you prefer English, here is a translation:

You shall not pervert justice, nor favor the rich or the poor; with justice you shall judge your people. Do not walk around gossiping among your people and do not stand by the blood of your fellow, I am G-d. Do not hate your brother in your heart; rebuke your nation and do not bear sin on their account. Do not take revenge, nor bear a grudge against the members of your people; love your fellow as yourself, I am G-d.

    What is the Torah teaching us? Do an oral narration on the above passage.

Month 3

Overview

Focus of the month: The books of במדבר - *Bamidbar* (Numbers) and דברים - *Devarim* (Deuteronomy)

Events: the forty years the Jewish people spent in the desert

Time period: years 2448 - 2488 on the Jewish calendar (years 1311 - 1351 BCE)

Brief summary of the time period:

The Jewish people are traveling through the desert on the way to the Land of Canaan. They send out spies to scout out the land, but the spies bring back a negative report. The Jews cry and complain, and G-d decrees that they will have to spend forty years in the desert and only the next generation will be able to enter the land.

In the desert, the Jews travel at times and encamp at times. They are sustained by manna, and their water comes through miraculous events.

Towards the end of forty years, Moshe dies, and Yehoshua takes over as the leader. The new generation is ready to enter the Promised Land.

Brief overview of books of the Tanach that are the focus of this month:

- במדבר

    Bamidbar (Numbers) - fourth book of the Torah and of the Tanach; covers the journey through the desert

- דברים

    Devarim (Deuteronomy) - fifth and final book of the Torah, fifth book of the Tanach; covers Moshe's final speech, review of the Torah taught by Moshe, Moshe's death, and Yehoshua's new role as the leader

Materials

Recommended reading for this month:
Little Midrash Says Bamidbar and *Little Midrash Says Devarim* or *A Treasury of Torah Aggados*, volume 4 (starting with chapter 36)
The Desert Diary by Gadi Pollack

Additional reading:
Shpeter by Rabbi Meir Uri Gottesman

Weekly reading:
Week 1: *The Desert Diary* by Gadi Pollack, pages 10 - 29
Week 2: *The Desert Diary* by Gadi Pollack, pages 29 - 54
Week 3: *The Desert Diary* by Gadi Pollack, pages 54 - 79
Week 4: Bamidbar (Numbers) 13:1-33

Grammar: *Grammar Land* by M. L. Nesbitt

Chapters 5: Sergeant Parsing's Visit to Schoolroom-shire; and 6: Mr. Adjective

Geography:
Map #4. The Land of Israel and the Transjordan
Map work:
- trace the route the Jewish people took on approach to the Land of Israel
- color the portions of the tribes of Reuven, Gad, and half of Menashe in three different colors

Music: *Ein Od Milvado by Yaakov Shwekey and Shlomi Shabat*: https://www.amazon.com/Milvado-Live-feat-Shlomi-Shabat/dp/B00CVEXDUW

Art: The Mishkan — exhibit at https://www.templeinstitute.org/mishkan.htm

Poetry: Song of Haazinu in Devarim 32:1-43

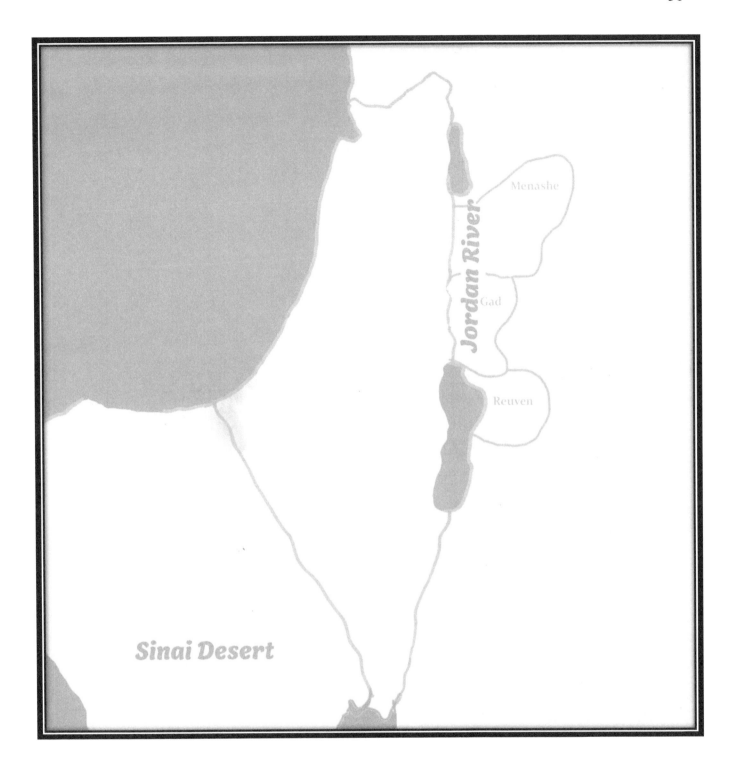

Map #4. The Land of Israel and the Transjordan

Week 1

From: *The Desert Diary*, by Gadi Pollack, page 15

Copy work/dictation passage:

It is fitting to begin my chronicle describing a glorious phenomenon we experience constantly, the Ananei haKavod. These Clouds of Glory surround us from all sides. They protect us from the oppressive heat of the day and the raw desert chill of the night. The Clouds even wash our clothing and delight us with a beautiful aroma.

Underline all nouns, circle all pronouns, and put squares around all articles.

Week 2

From: *The Desert Diary*, by Gadi Pollack, pages 36-37

Copy work/dictation passage:

A startling thing happened today. After all of the years of encampment here, at sunrise this morning the Cloud rose up from over the Mishkan. This was the sign to us that we are to begin traveling. We are to travel south, yet further from the Land of Canaan, but we understand that this is another step to reach our Land. We, the camp of Yehudah, acted quickly, as we are the first to journey. We packed and prepared to leave; for the first time in my life, I put shoes on my feet! While we were hurrying to wrap everything up, we heard the call of the special silver trumpets: Tekiah! Teruah! Tekiah! And so began our travels.

Pay attention to punctuation. Underline all nouns, circle all pronouns, and put squares around all articles.

Week 3

From: *The Desert Diary*, by Gadi Pollack, page 54

Copy work/dictation passage:

On the eve of the ninth night of this month, the men dug graves and at night lay down to sleep in them, as they do every year. However, the following morning, all awoke alive! We were confused: had we erred in the sighting of the moon and perhaps sanctified the month before its time? The next night, the men again slept in the graves. In the morning, all awoke alive once more. Each night until the full moon, the men did the same. When we ascertained that not one of our men had died, we knew that the decree of the ninth night had finally been annulled. The nation rejoiced with great happiness.

Pay attention to punctuation. Underline all adjectives.

Week 4

    From: Bamidbar (Numbers) 13:1-33
    Copy work: Bamidbar (Numbers) 13:25-28

You can copy the text from a *chumash* (or from sefaria.org) in the original Hebrew. If you prefer English, here is a translation:

They returned from spying the land at the end of forty days. And they went, and they came to Moshe and Aharon and to the whole congregation of children of Israel to the Paran desert at Kadesh and brought back to them a report, and to the whole congregation, and they showed them the fruit of the land. And they told him, and they said, "We came to the land to which you sent us, and it is also flowing with milk and honey, and this is its fruit. But the nation that lives in the land is very strong, and their cities are greatly fortified, and we saw there children of giants."

Do an oral narration of the passage. Which words seem extra here?

Month 4

Overview

Focus of the month: The books of יהושע - *Yehoshua* (Joshua), שופטים - *Shoftim* (Judges), and רות - Rus (Ruth)

Events: the conquest of the Land of Israel under the leadership of Yehoshua and life in the land in the period of the Judges

Time period: years 2488 - 2830 on the Jewish calendar (years 1351 - 931 BCE)

Brief summary of the time period:

The Jewish people conquer the Land of Canaan, which now becomes the Land of Israel. They divide the land, and each tribe receives a portion. Yehoshua dies, and the Jewish people are governed by judges. The Jewish people strive to serve G-d, but keep reverting to idol worship. As a result, they find themselves attacked and persecuted by other nations. The judges must lead the nation to war. The Jews repent and miraculously win the war, but too soon the cycle repeats itself.

Brief overview of books of the Tanach that are the focus of this month:

- יהושע

    Yehoshua (Joshua) - first book of the *Nevi'im Rishonim* (Early Prophets) and sixth book of the Tanach; covers the conquest of the Land of Israel through death of Yehoshua

- שופטים

    Shoftim (Judges) - second book of the *Nevi'im Rishonim* (Early Prophets) and seventh book of the Tanach; covers the period of the Judges

- רות

    Rus (Ruth) - one of the five *megillos* (scrolls) and the eighteenth book of the Tanach; read on Shavuos in some synagogues; tells the story of the righteous convert Rus, the great-grandmother of King David; the story took place during the period of the Judges

Materials

Recommended reading for this month:
Little Midrash Says Yehoshua and Family Midrash Says Shoftim or *A Treasury of Aggados on Nach*, volume 1, parts 1 and 2

Weekly reading:
Week 1: Yehoshua (Joshua) 2:1-24
Week 2: *Three Hundred Men* from the book *The Prisoner and Other Tales of Faith* by Rabbi Salomon Alter Halpern
Week 3: Book of Ruth (Artscroll children's edition highly recommended)
Week 4: *The Girl from Moav* from the book *The Prisoner and Other Tales of Faith* by Rabbi Salomon Alter Halpern

Grammar: *Grammar Land* by M. L. Nesbitt
Chapters 7: Mr. Adjective Tried for Stealing; and 8: The Quarrel

Geography:

Map #5. The Land of Israel
Map work: label each portion of the land with the name of the tribe that received it

Music: Rabbi Levi Sudri on the Book of Yehoshua: http://www.levisudri.com/songs_en.php

Art: *The Seven Trumpets of Jericho* by James Tissot: https://upload.wikimedia.org/wikipedia/commons/0/0d/Tissot_The_Seven_Trumpets_of_Jericho.jpg

Poetry: Song of Devorah in Shoftim (Judges) 5:1-31

Map #5. The Land of Israel

Week 1

    From: Yehoshua (Joshua) chapter 2
    Copy work/dictation passage: Yehoshua (Joshua) 2:15-16

    You can copy the text from a *Tanach* (or from sefaria.org) in the original Hebrew.
    If you prefer English, here is a translation:

And she lowered them on a rope through the window, because her house was in the wall of the fortification, and she lived in the fortification. And she said to them, "Go to the mountain, so that the pursuers would not meet you, and hide yourselves there for three days, until the pursuers return, and afterward, go on your way.

    Do an oral narration of the passage.

Week 2

From: *Three Hundred Men*, from the book *The Prisoner and Other Tales of Faith* by Rabbi Salomon Alter Halpern

Copy work/dictation passage:

The sun had risen, when he felt that someone was watching him. He peered out — keeping in the shade of the wine-press entrance. No one to be seen. But wait — under that tree… A moment ago he hadn't seen anything there, but now — yes, there was a man, sitting quite still, looking at him… Gideon felt uneasy. How had the man got there so suddenly — if he was a man and not some kind of spirit? But he felt he had to go to him. Still the man did not move; but when Gideon had come quite near him, the man lifted his hand and spoke: "G-d with you, mighty warrior!"

Pay attention to punctuation.

Week 3

From: The Artscroll Children's Book of Ruth (1:16-17)

Copy work/dictation:

Ruth said, "Don't beg me to leave you. Wherever you go, I will go. Wherever you stay, I will stay. Your people are my people. Your G-d is my G-d. Where you die, I will die, and I will be buried there. May Hashem do this to me and even more, if anything but death will ever separate us."

Pay attention to punctuation. Do an oral narration of the passage.

Week 4

From: *The Girl from Moav*, from the book *The Prisoner and Other Tales of Faith* by Rabbi Salomon Alter Halpern

Copy work/dictation passage:

"No," answered Naomi. "I really thought so then. We all did. But after we came back I heard that the prophets had been here and taught us an oral law which had been forgotten. They said they knew positively that only men of Ammon and Mo'ab are forbidden to marry Israelite women, but that a Moabite woman, like you, can marry any man of Israel. The people are not used to the idea yet, but Bo'az is a learned man. He will be only too glad to be the first to demonstrate the law, and the Elders will back him up."

Pay attention to punctuation. Underline all adjective-pronouns.

Month 5

Overview

Focus of the month: The books of שמואל - *Shmuel Alef and Beis* (Samuel I and II), and תהילים - *Tehillim* (Psalms)

Events: the reigns of Shaul, the first Jewish king, and David, the first king from the tribe of Yehuda

Time period: years 2830 - 2924 on the Jewish calendar (years 931 - 837 BCE)

Brief summary of the time period:

Shmuel becomes the last Judge of Israel. The Jewish people request a king. With divine guidance, Shmuel appoints Shaul from the tribe of Binyamin as the first Jewish king. At first, Shaul's reign is successful, but eventually he makes too many mistakes. Shmuel appoints David as the next king. Shaul attempts to kill David, who flees and collects his own army. Shaul makes several attempts to pursue David but fails to capture him. Then Shaul is killed in battle, and David takes over the throne. He leads the Jewish people wisely and justly and defeats numerous enemies of the Jews.

Brief overview of books of the Tanach that are the focus of this month:

- שמואל

   Shmuel Alef and *Beis* (Samuel I and II) - third book of the *Nevi'im Rishonim* (Early Prophets) and eighth book of the Tanach; covers the reigns of King Shaul and King David

- תהילים

   Tehillim (Psalms) - first book of the *Kesuvim* (Writings) and fourteenth book of the Tanach; a collection of psalms attributed to King David

Materials

Recommended reading for this month:

Family Midrash Says Shmuel Alef and *Family Midrash Says Shmuel Beis* or *A Treasury of Aggados on Nach*, volume 1, parts 3, 4, and 5

Artscroll Children's Tehillim

Additional reading:

Elementary:

Dovid Hamelech by Rabbi Nachman Seltzer

Weekly reading:

Week 1: *To Rule the Land* by Yehudis Litvak

Week 2: Shmuel Alef (Samuel I) 17:1-54

Week 3: *On the Run* by Yehudis Litvak

Week 4: *King David's Coins* by Nissan Mindel (available online, free of charge, at https://www.chabad.org/library/article_cdo/aid/111926/jewish/King-Davids-Coins.htm)

Grammar: *Grammar Land* by M. L. Nesbitt
Chapters 9: Dr. Verb; and 10: Dr. Verb's Three Tenses, Number, and Person

Geography:
Map #6. The land of Israel
Map work: find and circle Jerusalem

Music: harp music by Shoshanna Harrari: https://www.youtube.com/watch?v=mg6oLtqfWvA and https://www.harrariharps.com/

Art: Baruch Nachshon (https://nachshonart.com); especially relevant to this time period is his illustrated *Tehillim* (Psalms) (https://nachshonart.com/product/psalms-tehillim/)

Poetry: *Tehillim* (Psalm) 23 (translation and commentaries available in *Artscroll Children's Tehillim*)

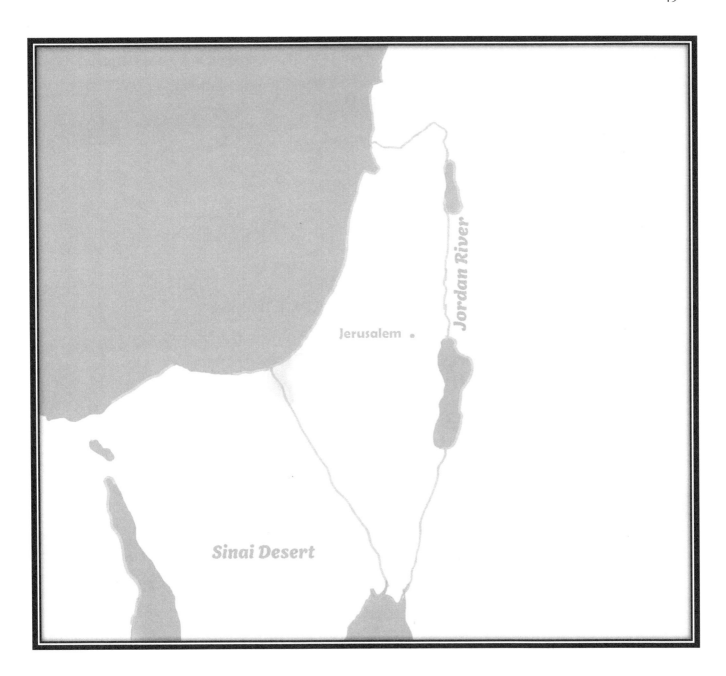

Map #6. The Land of Israel

Week 1

From: *To Rule the Land*, by Yehudis Litvak

Copy work/dictation passage:

At the workshop, Achiram put aside all thoughts of kings and focused on his work. First, he brought in water from the well, then cleaned the kiln, preparing it for the day's batch of pottery. His father was busy looking over the jars he'd fired in the kiln the day before. He picked two large jars and wrapped them in a piece of cloth.

Underline all verbs.

Week 2

    From: Shmuel Alef (Samuel I) chapter 17
    Copy work/dictation passage: Shmuel Alef (Samuel I) 17:48-50

You can copy the text from a *Tanach* (or from sefaria.org) in the original Hebrew. If you prefer English, here is a translation:

And it was, when the Philistine rose and approached David, that David hurried and ran to the battle line towards the Philistine. And David reached into the bag and took out a stone from it, and he slung it and hit the Philistine on his forehead, and the stone sunk into his forehead, and he fell on his face to the ground. And David overpowered the Philistine with a slingshot and a stone; he struck the Philistine down and he killed him, and there was no sword in David's hand.

    Do an oral narration of this passage.

Week 3

From: *On the Run*, by Yehudis Litvak

Copy work/dictation passage:

Inside, it took Nachshon a few moments to get used to the darkness, illuminated slightly by several oil lamps. When his eyes got used to the dim light, he saw that the cave was full of men – hundreds of them. Some were talking, others eating, and others dozing. Their robes were fraying, their shoes worn. Somebody sat near the wall of the cave, bent over a scroll. Another man was playing a small harp.

Choose a verb from this passage and determine its person, number, and tense.

Week 4

From: *King David's Coins* by Nissan Mindel (available online, free of charge, at https://www.chabad.org/library/article_cdo/aid/111926/jewish/King-Davids-Coins.htm)

Copy work/dictation passage:

The ministers went to work and before long, off came shiny new coins of gold and silver. Everybody was anxious to see and own the new coins, for they were honest and had their full weight. The coins spread to other lands too, for merchants would have David's coins rather than any others.

Choose a verb from the passage and conjugate it.

Month 6

Overview

Focus of the month: The books of מלכים - *Melachim Alef and Beis* (Kings I and II), משלי - *Mishlei* (Proverbs), קהלת - *Koheles* (Ecclesiastes), שיר השירים - *Shir Hashirim* (Song of Songs), יונה - *Yonah* (Book of Jonah), and ישיהו - *Yeshayahu* (Isaiah).

Events: the period of kings, from King Shlomo through the exile of the ten tribes of the Northern Kingdom

Time period: years 2924 - 3205 on the Jewish calendar (years 837 - 556 BCE)

Brief summary of the time period:

King David dies and King Shlomo ascends to the throne. Under his leadership, the Jewish kingdom grows and prospers. King Shlomo builds the Temple in Jerusalem and makes peace with the surrounding nations. He becomes known throughout the world for his exceptional wisdom.

After King Shlomo's death, his son Rechavam becomes the next king. Rechavam doesn't measure up to his father, and the Jewish kingdom splits into two, Yehuda and Yisrael. Over the next two centuries, both kingdoms experience physical and spiritual ups and downs, sometimes uniting for a common cause and other times fighting among each other. Eventually, the Northern Kingdom of Yisrael is captured by Sancheriv, king of Ashur, and its population is exiled and scattered throughout the world. The prophet Yeshayahu is active during this time period, as well as the minor prophets Hoshea, Amos, Micha, and Ovadia, whose short prophecies are part of the *Trei Asar* (the Twelve Minor Prophets), which will discuss in more detail next month.

Brief overview of books of the Tanach that are the focus of this month:

- מלכים

Melachim Alef and *Beis* (Kings I and II) - fourth book of the *Nevi'im Rishonim* (Early Prophets) and ninth book of the Tanach; covers the period of the Kings, from the end of King David's reign through the destruction and exile of the Southern Kingdom of Yehuda

- משלי

Mishlei (Proverbs) - second book of the *Kesuvim* (Writings) and fifteenth book of the Tanach; a collection of proverbs attributed to King Shlomo

- קהלת

Koheles (Ecclesiastes) - one of the five *megillos* (scrolls) and the twentieth book of the Tanach; words of wisdom attributed to King Shlomo

- שיר השירים

Shir Hashirim (Song of Songs) - one of the five *megillos* (scrolls) and the seventeenths book of the Tanach; a song expressing love between G-d and the Jewish people, attributed to King Shlomo

- יונה

Yonah (Jonah) - one of the books of the Trei Asar (Twelve Minor Prophets), which is the thirteenth book of the Tanach; the story of the prophet Yonah whom G-d sent to the city of Nineveh to urge the residents to repent

- ישיהו

Yeshayahu (Isaiah) - first book of the *Neviim Achronim* (Later Prophets) and the tenth book of the Tanach; Prophet Yeshayahu's prophecy urging the Jewish people to repent at the time of the Kings and warning about the upcoming exile of the Ten Tribes

Materials

Recommended reading for this month:

Family Midrash Says Melachim Alef and *Family Midrash Says Melachim Beis* (pages 5 - 345) or *A Treasury of Aggados on Nach*, volume 2 and volume 3 part 10

Book of Yonah (Jonah), Artscroll Children's edition recommended

The Miracles of Elisha by Sterna Citron

The Prophet Isaiah by Nissan Mindel (available online, free of charge, at https://www.chabad.org/library/article_cdo/aid/112071/jewish/The-Prophet-Isaiah.htm)

Additional reading:
Elementary:
The Secret Tunnel by Joy Nelkin Wieder
Middle grades/high school:
Lamp of Darkness by Dave Mason and Mike Feuer

Weekly reading:
Week 1: *The Miracles of Elisha* by Sterna Citron, pages 10-23
Week 2: *The Miracles of Elisha* by Sterna Citron, pages 24-57
Week 3: *The Miracles of Elisha* by Sterna Citron, pages 58-83
Week 4: Book of Yonah (Jonah), Artscroll Children's edition recommended

Grammar: *Grammar Land* by M. L. Nesbitt
Chapters 11: Sergeant Parsing in Schoolroom-shire Again; and 12: The Nominative Case

Geography:
Map #7. The kingdoms of Yehuda and Yisrael in the Land of Israel
Map work:
  label the Northern and Southern kingdoms
  find and circle their capitals, Jerusalem and Shomron

Music: *Lakol Zman* by Uri Davidi (https://www.amazon.com/Lakol-Zman/dp/B01BN14PS2)
Art: *Sacred Vessels and Vestments of the Holy Temple* exhibition at the Temple Institute; available online at https://www.templeinstitute.org/gallery.htm
Poetry: *Koheles* (Ecclesiastes) 3:1-8

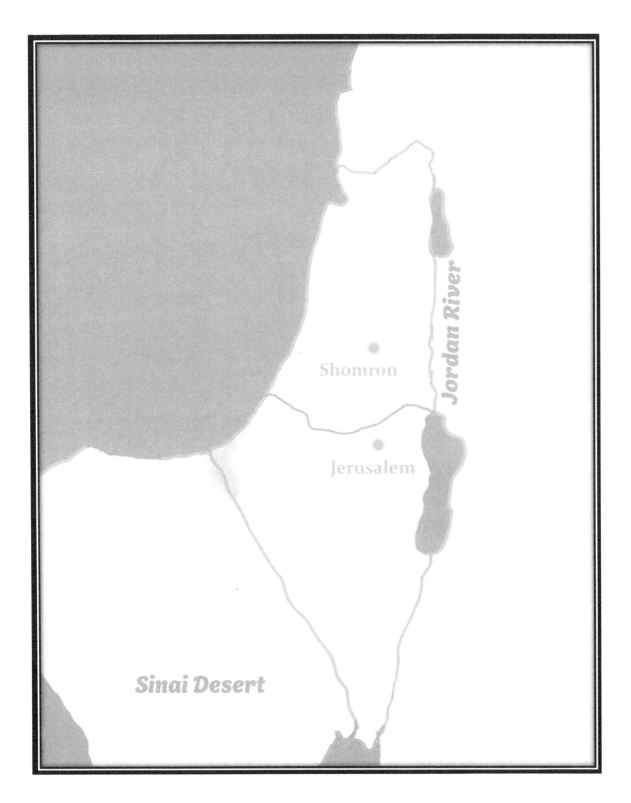

Map #7. The Kingdoms of Yehuda and Yisrael in the Land of Israel

Week 1

    From: *The Miracles of Elisha* by Sterna Citron, pages 10-23

Copy work/dictation passage (page 13):

*   Happiest of all was Elisha. A couple of hours ago, he was the son of a farmer, plowing with his father's oxen, and now he was going to serve Eliyahu and learn from him. Eliyahu would show him how to truly love and fear G-d and would teach him how to take care of the Jewish people. How thankful Elisha was!*

Underline all verbs that consist of more than one word.

Week 2

From: *The Miracles of Elisha* by Sterna Citron, pages 24-57

Copy work/dictation passage (page 35):

She brought the pots home and carefully closed the door behind her and the children, just as the prophet had told her. She held the small jug with the olive oil in her hand while her children brought her the first pot. As she began pouring, a miracle happened. The empty pot quickly filled up to the top with bright, shiny olive oil!

Underline all verbs, then choose one verb and conjugate it.

Week 3

From: *The Miracles of Elisha* by Sterna Citron, pages 58-83

Copy work/dictation passage (page 65):

After a few months of peace, the king of Aram sent his army to surround the capital city of Shomron. The enemy would not let the Jewish people go in or out of the city. Farmers could not come into the city to sell their crops. There was hardly any food. The people of Shomron were starving.

Underline all the nominative cases with one line, and all the verbs that agree with them with two lines.

Week 4

 From: Book of Yonah (Jonah) — Artscroll Children's edition recommended

 Copy work/dictation passage: Yonah (Jonah) 1:3-4

You can copy the text from a *Tanach* (or from sefaria.org) in the original Hebrew. If you prefer English, here is the Artscroll Children's edition translation:

 Yonah got up and fled to Tarshish as if to get away from Hashem. He went to Yaffo, and found a boat there going to Tarshish. He paid the fare and went onto the boat to go with them to Tarshish running away from Hashem. Then Hashem caused a mighty wind to blow on the sea. It became such a huge storm on the sea that it seemed as if the boat would be destroyed.

 Do an oral narration of the passage.

Month 7

Overview

This is the seventh month of the homeschooling year. If you are beginning your year in the fall, you will be busy preparing for Pesach (see our *Jewish Year Curriculum Guide* for more details).

Even if you begin your year in a different month, you might want to slow down and reassess how the learning is going, or you might want to review what you covered in the previous months. Therefore, for this month, we prepared only three weeks of learning. As always, if you find yourself with extra time, please see our recommendations for additional reading.

Focus of the month: The books of מלכים ב - *Melachim Beis* (Kings II), ירמיהו - *Yirmiyahu* (Jeremiah), איכה - *Eicha* (Lamentations), תרי עשר - Trei Assar (Twelve Minor Prophets)

Events: the period of kings, from the exile of the ten tribes of the Northern Kingdom to the beginning of the Babylonian exile

Time period: years 3205 - 3338 on the Jewish calendar (years 556 - 423 BCE)

Brief summary of the time period:

After the ten tribes of the Northern Kingdom are exiled, only the two tribes of Yehuda and Binyamin, as well as *leviyim* and *kohanim* who lived in their territory, remain in Eretz Yisrael and maintain their independence in the Southern Kingdom. At first, the kingdom does well under the rule of the righteous King Chizkiyahu, but his son Menashe brings an idol into the Temple and persecutes the faithful Jews. His grandson, Yoshiyahu, restores the glory of the Jewish kingdom and renovates the Temple, but his children and grandchildren put the kingdom in jeopardy when the Babylonian king Nevuchadnetzar threatens the Jewish kingdom. They refuse to accept his rule, but Nevuchadnetzar overpowers them, exiles the Jews from their land, and eventually destroys the Temple. The prophet Yirmiyahu is active in this time period, along with the minor prophets Yoel, Nachum, Chavakuk, and Tzefania, whose short prophecies are part of the *Trei Asar* (the Twelve Minor Prophets).

Brief overview of books of the Tanach that are the focus of this month:

- מלכים

Melachim Beis (Kings II) - fourth book of the *Nevi'im Rishonim* (Early Prophets) and ninth book of the Tanach; covers the period of the Kings

- ירמיהו

Yirmiyahu (Jeremiah) - second book of the *Neviim Achronim* (Later Prophets) and the eleventh book of the Tanach; Prophet Yirmiyahu's dire warnings to the Jewish people

איכה -

Eicha (Lamentations) - one of the five *megillos* (scrolls), which is read in synagogues on Tisha B'Av, and the nineteenth book of the Tanach; Prophet Yirmiyahu's prophecy about the destruction of the Temple and exile

תרי עשר -

Trei Assar (Twelve Minor Prophets) - twelve short prophecies compiled into one book; contains prophecies by Hoshea (Hosea), Yoel (Joel), Amos, Ovadia (Obadiah), Yona (Jonah), Micha (Mica), Nachum (Nahum), Chavakuk (Habakkuk), Tzefania (Zephaniah), Chaggai (Haggai), Zecharia (Zechariah), and Malachi

Materials

Recommended reading for this month:

*Family Midrash Says Melachim Beis (*pages 345 - 399) or *A Treasury of Aggados on Nach*, volume 3, part 12

The Prophet Jeremiah by Nissan Mindel (available online, free of charge, at https://www.chabad.org/library/article_cdo/aid/469488/jewish/Jeremiah.htm)

Weekly reading:

Week 1: *When We Left Yerushalayim* by Genendel Krohn (part 1)

Week 2: *Yirmiyahu* (Jeremiah) 36:1-32

Week 3: *Follow His Word* from the book *Ripples in Time* by Brocha Miller

Grammar: *Grammar Land* by M. L. Nesbitt
Chapters 13: Adverb; and 14: Preposition

Geography:
Map #8. Babylon and the Land of Israel
Map work: trace the route from Eretz Yisrael to Bavel (Babylon)

Music: *Mama Rochel* by Abie Rotenberg (song #4 in the *Journeys IV* album)

Art: *The Prophet Jeremiah* by Marc Chagall (https://en.wikipedia.org/wiki/Marc_Chagall#/media/File:The_Prophet_Jeremiah_-_1968_-Wull.jpg)

Poetry: *Eicha* (Lamentations 1:1-8)

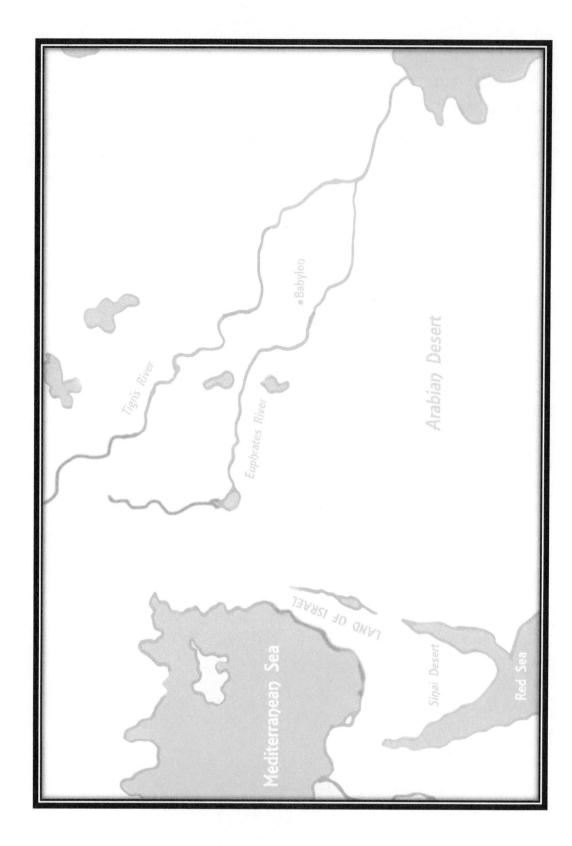

Map #8. Babylon and the Land of Israel (Eretz Yisrael)

Week 1

From: *When We Left Yerushalayim* by Genendel Krohn, pages 5-20

Copy work/dictation passage (page 15):

Thousands of Jews walked together sadly, with their heads down. Around them were hundreds of soldiers, making sure that no one tried to run away. The Jewish people, once rich and important, were now hungry, tired, and barefoot. They were taken like prisoners from the land they loved so much. Tears rolled down their cheeks, but they could not wipe them away because their hands were tied up in chains.

Pay attention to punctuation. Underline an adverb.

Week 2

> From: Yirmiyahu (Jeremiah) 36:1-32
> Copy work/dictation passage: Yirmiyahu (Jeremiah) 36:4-7

You can copy the text from a *Tanach* (or from sefaria.org) in the original Hebrew. If you prefer English, here is a translation:

And Yirmiyahu called for Baruch ben Neriah, and Baruch wrote from the mouth of Yirmiyahu all the words of Hashem Who spoke to him on a scroll. And Yirmiyahu commanded Baruch, saying, "I am detained; I am unable to go to the House of Hashem. You go and read the scroll that you wrote from my mouth, the words of Hashem into the ears of the people of the House of Hashem on a fast day, and also in the ears of all Jews that come from their cities — you shall read to them."

Our Sages tell us that this scroll was *Megillas Eicha* (the *Book of Lamentations*). Do an oral narration of the passage.

Week 3

From: *Follow His Word* from the book *Ripples in Time* by Brocha Miller

Copy work/dictation passage:

At dinner, I taste the vegetables and barley cakes spread out on the rough table. After months of near starvation, I should be enjoying this. It is different from the court I'm used to, the company of this small group of farmers. Their blistered hands and weather-lined faces speak of labor and long hours in the sun. I look down at my own hands, once smooth and lily white, now chapped, the nails dirty and long. I've come a long way from the palace; I must remember that. I will stay here in this town of soldiers and laborers, and I will make sure we will survive.

Pay attention to punctuation. Underline all prepositions.

Month 8

Overview

This is the eighth month of the homeschooling year. If you are beginning your year in the fall, you will be busy celebrating Pesach (see our *Jewish Year Curriculum Guide* for more details).

Even if you begin your year in a different month, you might want to slow down and reassess how the learning is going, or you might want to review what you covered in the previous months. Therefore, for this month, we prepared only three weeks of learning. As always, if you find yourself with extra time, please see our recommendations for additional reading.

Focus of the month: The books of דניאל - *Daniel* (Daniel), יחזקל - *Yechezkel* (Ezekiel)

Events: life in Bavel (Babylonia) under the Babylonian kings

Time period: years 3338 - 3395 on the Jewish calendar (years 423 - 366 BCE)

Brief summary of the time period:

The exiles from the Kingdom of Yehuda settle in Bavel (Babylonia), and later scatter throughout the empire. They learn to live in exile, and some Jews are appointed to high positions in the royal court. Despite persecution, and sometimes threats to life due to their commitment to their own religion, the Jews manage to grow and prosper and gain respect of their rulers.

Brief overview of books of the Tanach that are the focus of this month:

- דניאל

Daniel (Daniel) - the ninth book of the *Kesuvim* (Writings) and the twenty second book of the Tanach; covers most of the Babylonian exile

- יחזקל

Yechezkel (Ezekiel) - the third book of the *Neviim Achronim* (Later Prophets) and the twelfth book of the Tanach; Prophet Yechezkel's prophecy about the destruction of the Temple and about the rebuilding of the future Temple

Materials

Recommended reading for this month:

Family Midrash Says Daniel (Part 1 and pages 383-389) or *A Treasury of Aggados on Nach*, volume 3, part 11

The Prophet Ezekiel by Nissan Mindel (available online, free of charge, at https://www.chabad.org/library/article_cdo/aid/4035701/jewish/The-Prophet-Ezekiel.htm)

Additional reading:
Middle grades/high school:
The Decree by Rebbetzin Sarah Feldbrand

Weekly reading:
Week 1: *Foreign Soil* by Yehudis Litvak
Week 2: Yechezkel (Ezekiel) 36:22-38
Week 3: *The Return* by Yehudis Litvak

Grammar: *Grammar Land* by M. L. Nesbitt

Chapters 15: Prepositions Govern the Objective Case; and 16: Conjunction

Geography:
Map #9. Mesopotamia
Map work: mark Bavel (Babylon), where the Jewish community was exiled

Music: Babylonian Jewish music (samples available at http://www.bjhcenglish.com/music)
Art: *Belshazzar's Feast* by Rembrandt (https://en.wikipedia.org/wiki/Rembrandt#/media/File:Rembrandt_-_Belshazzar%27s_Feast_-_WGA19123.jpg)
Poetry: Yechezkel (Ezekiel) 11:17-24

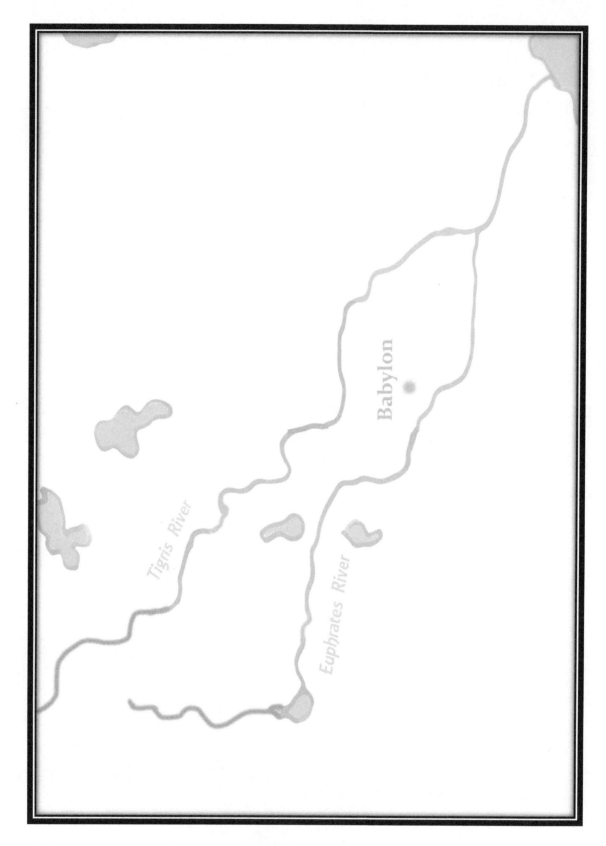

Map #9. Mesopotamia

Week 1

From: *Foreign Soil* by Yehudis Litvak

Copy work/dictation passage:

With a pounding heart Matanya walked into the mesivta *the following Shabbos. The small room was full of people, some learning in groups, others in pairs, and yet others on their own. It took Matanya a minute to spot Benayahu, who looked very different in his white Shabbos robe and turban than he'd looked in his mud-encrusted work clothes at the construction site. He had an almost regal air around him as he stood in front of a small group, speaking to them. Matanya realized that Benayahu had been too modest – he'd neglected to tell him that he was not only learning, but also teaching at the* mesivta.

Underline prepositions that govern objective cases with one line and the objective cases themselves with two lines.

Week 2

> From: Yechezkel (Ezekiel) 36:22-38
> Copy work/dictation passage: Yechezkel (Ezekiel) 36:24-27

You can copy the text from a *Tanach* (or from sefaria.org) in the original Hebrew. If you prefer English, here is a translation:

And I will take you from among the nations, and I will gather you from all the lands, and I will bring you to your land. And I will sprinkle you with pure water and you'll be purified from all your impurities and from all your idols; I will purify you. And I will give you a new heart and a new spirit I will put within you; I will remove the heart of stone from your flesh and give you a heart of flesh.

Do an oral narration. What is this passage about?

Week 3

From: *The Return* by Yehudis Litvak

Copy work/dictation passage:

Finally, after months of traveling, Zerubavel announced that they were approaching Eretz Yisrael. They were out of the desert now, and the road was lined with grass and occasional trees. It sloped up and down small hills. Achikam looked ahead, curious to see the land he had heard so much about.

Underline all conjunctions.

Month 9

Overview

Focus of the month: The Book of אסתר - Esther
Events: life in exile under Persian rule
Time period: years 3338 - 3395 on the Jewish calendar (years 423 - 366 BCE)

Brief summary of the time period:

Persia becomes the next world power after the fall of Babylon. Its king, Achashverosh, rules over a large empire, including all the lands where Jews have settled. He marries Esther, a Jewish orphan who was raised by her cousin, the sage and Jewish leader Mordechai. Esther keeps her identity hidden from Achashverosh. Influenced by his evil adviser, Haman, Achashverosh issues a decree permitting the annihilation of the whole Jewish community. Esther risks her life to reveal her identity and plead for the Jews. Achashverosh executes Haman and allows the Jews to fight back. The Jews destroy their enemies and save their community.

Brief overview of books of the Tanach that are the focus of this month:

- אסתר

Esther - one of the five *megillos* and the twenty first book of the Tanach; covers the reign of King Achashverosh of Persia and the story of Purim

Materials

Recommended reading for this month:
The Complete Story of Purim by Nissan Mindel or *A Treasury of Aggados on Nach*, volume 4, part 13
Artscroll Children's Megillah

Additional reading:
Middle grades/high school:
The Gilded Cage by Sorale Brownstein

Weekly reading:
Week 1: *Palace Intrigue* from the book *Ripples in Time* by Brocha Miller
Week 2: *The Beginning* from the book *The Prisoner and Other Tales of Faith* by Rabbi Salomon Asher Halpern
Week 3: *No Sleep That Night* from the book *The Prisoner and Other Tales of Faith* by Rabbi Salomon Asher Halpern
Week 4: *Megillas Esther* (Book of Esther) — Artscroll Children's Megillah recommended

Grammar: *Grammar Land* by M. L. Nesbitt
　　Chapters 17: Active Verbs Govern the Objective Case; and 18: The Possessive Case

Geography:
　　Map #10. The Persian Empire
　　Map work:
　　　　Color in King Achashverosh's empire, from Hodu to Kush (India to Ethiopia)
　　　　Mark Shushan (Susa), where the story of Purim took place

Music: *Shoshanat Ya'akov* by Shlomo Katz (song #4 in the Yismach Melech album: https://music.amazon.com/albums/B01B73U56C/B01B73UBWU/CATALOG)

Art: Glazed brick relief from the royal palace in Shushan (Susa): https://www.gettyimages.com/detail/news-photo/glazed-brick-relief-of-archers-from-the-royal-guard-palace-news-photo/501578277#glazed-brick-relief-of-archers-from-the-royal-guard-palace-of-darius-picture-id501578277. (Many other images of artifacts from this time period appear in Rabbi Yehuda Landy's book *Purim and the Persian Empire*.)

Poetry: *Shoshanat Yaakov* (original Hebrew and English translation available at http://www.zemirotdatabase.org/view_song.php?id=202)

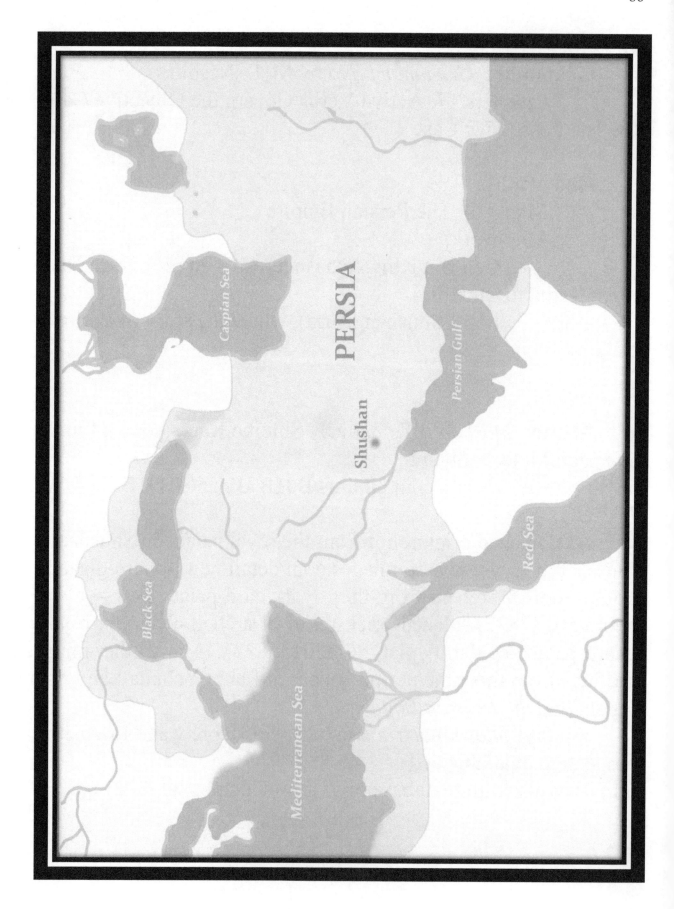

Map #10. The Persian Empire

Week 1

From: *The Palace Intrigue*, from the book *Ripples in Time* by Brocha Miller

Copy work/dictation passage:

I see a ribbon of turquoise between the branches, and I know I am not alone in my desire for quiet contemplation. My friend Miriam rests her blue sleeve against the tree trunk. Her job as Vashti's maid is as demanding as mine, yet we still find the time to meet and enjoy a few moments of talking, giggling, and daydreaming, as two young girls will do, whatever their position in the kingdom.

Underline all Objective cases.

Week 2

From: *The Beginning*, from the book *The Prisoner and Other Tales of Faith* by Rabbi Salomon Alter Halpern

Copy work/dictation passage:

Shaltiel was pondering over these words when he became aware of a new sound from afar, above the subdued murmurs from the market place. A wailing and crying, coming nearer, taken up by one voice after another. At last the procession reached the market place; at its head was an aged Rabbi, clad in sack-cloth. As he reached the torch light in the market place, Shaltiel recognized him: none other than "the Jewish Courtier," the famous Mordechai.

Pay attention to punctuation. Underline verbs with a single line and objective cases with a double line.

Week 3

From: *No Sleep That Night*, from the book *The Prisoner and Other Tales of Faith* by Rabbi Salomon Alter Halpern

Copy work/dictation passage:

Chananel's father hadn't even heard them. He had gone on ahead, his head bowed, thinking. So he didn't notice the litter stopping next to Chananel. Armazd's father stepped out, and paid off the slaves. Chananel saw at once that he had been drinking.

Underline all possessive cases.

Week 4

From: Megillas Esther (Book of Esther)

Copy work/dictation passage: Megillas Esther (Book of Esther) 8:15-16.

You can copy the text from a *Tanach* (or from sefaria.org) in the original Hebrew.

If you prefer English, here is the Artscroll Children's Megillah translation:

Mordechai left the palace wearing royal clothing that was colored blue and white. He had a large gold crown, and a robe made out of the finest linen and purple wool. And the city of Shushan rejoiced and was happy. The Jews enjoyed light and happiness, joy and honor.

Do an oral narration. What was the turnaround in the story?

Month 10

Overview

This is the last month in this time period, and you might want to go over and review what you have learned. We prepared only three weeks of materials. During the last week, you can focus on what you feel needs more attention in the material we've covered. You can also do additional grammar exercises of your choice. Free grammar materials and exercises can be found at https://www.kissgrammar.org.

Focus of the month: The book of עזרא/נחמיה - Ezra/Nechemia (Nehemiah)

Events: return to the Land of Israel and rebuilding of the Second Temple

Time period: years 3395-3410 on the Jewish calendar (years 366-350 BCE)

Brief summary of the time period:

King Koresh (Cyrus the Great) of Persia gives the exiled Jews permission to return to Eretz Yisrael and to rebuild the Temple. A small group of Jews, headed by Zerubavel, returns and begins construction, but Koresh, influenced by the Samaritans who had taken over the land during the exile, orders to halt the construction. Eighteen years later, King Daryavesh (Darius) allows the Jews to finish rebuilding the Temple. A larger group of Jews, led by Ezra, returns to Eretz Yisrael, but they still encounter difficulties from their neighbors. Nechemia, the king's cup bearer, comes to Jerusalem and restores order. The Jews continue to rebuild their country, though it remains a province of Persia. The prophets Chaggai, Zecharia, and Malachi are active in this time period. Their short prophecies are part of the *Trei Asar* (the Twelve Minor Prophets).

Brief overview of books of the Tanach that are the focus of this month:

- עזרא/נחמיה

Ezra/Nechemia (Ezra/Nehemiah) - the twenty third book of the Tanach; covers the rebuilding of the Second Temple and the return of Jews to Eretz Yisrael.

- דיברי הימים

Divrei Hayamim (Chronicles) - the twenty fourth, and last, book of the Tanach, that summarizes the story of the Jewish people throughout the time period of the Tanach.

Materials

Recommended reading for this month:
Ezra the Scribe by Nissan Mindel (available online, free of charge, at https://www.chabad.org/library/article_cdo/aid/111905/jewish/Ezra-the-Scribe.htm) or A Treasury of Aggados on Nach, volume 4, part 14

Weekly reading:
Week 1: *Chaggai* (Haggai) 1:1-2:9
Week 2: *Music for the Soul* by Yehudis Litvak
Week 3: *Building the Wall* by Yehudis Litvak

Grammar: Review exercises of your choice. See https://www.kissgrammar.org/ for free exercises.

Geography:
Map #11. Eretz Yisrael and Mesopotamia
Map work:

trace the journey of the Jews from exile back to Eretz Yisrael

mark Jerusalem

Music: *Veheishiv Lev Avos* by Avraham Fried - song # 6 in the Melave Malka album: http://jewishmusic.fm/album/melave-malka/

Art: *Nehemiah Views the Ruins of Jerusalem Walls* by Gustave Dore: https://en.wikipedia.org/wiki/Nehemiah#/media/File:108.Nehemiah_Views_the_Ruins_of_Jerusalem%27s_Walls.jpg

Poetry: Malachi 3:1-6

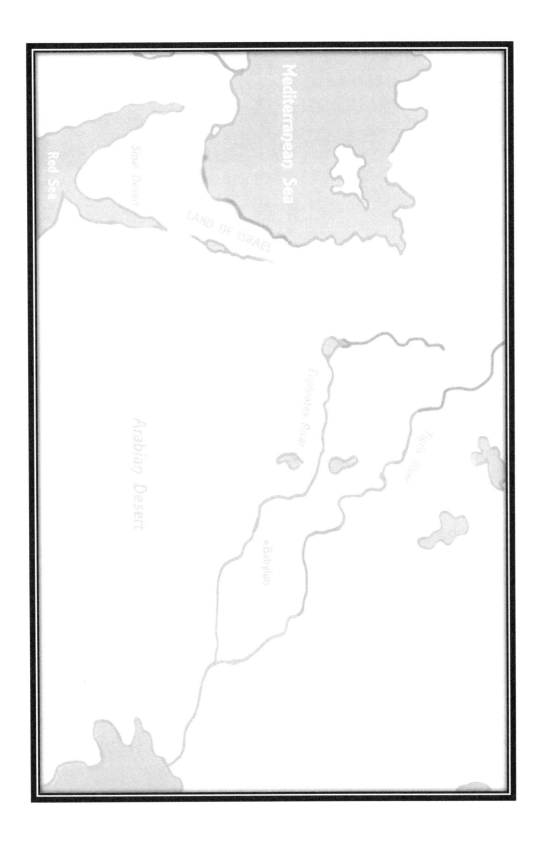

Map #11. The Land of Israel (Eretz Yisrael) and Mesopotamia

Week 1

> From: Chaggai (Haggai) 1:1-2:9
> Copy work/dictation passage: Chaggai (Haggai) 1:14-15

You can copy the text from a *Tanach* (or from sefaria.org) in the original Hebrew. If you prefer English, here is a translation:

> *G-d aroused the spirit of Zerubavel, son of Shaltiel, the governor of Yehuda, and the spirit of Yehoshua, the son of Yehotzaddok, the High Priest, and the spirit of the entire remnant of the people, and they came and did work on the House of G-d of Legions, their G-d. On the twenty-fourth day of the sixth month, in the second year of King Daryavesh.*

Do an oral narration of the passage. When did this take place, relative to what happened before?

Week 2

From: *Music for the Soul* by Yehudis Litvak

Copy work/dictation passage:

On the first day of the month of Nisan, Shmuel went to see Gershom off. His heart felt heavy as he watched the assembled crowd — over a thousand people — waving goodbye to family members and friends who were remaining in Bavel.

Label each word in the passage with its part of speech.

Week 3

From: *Building the Wall* by Yehudis Litvak

Copy work/dictation passage:

Together, they began to move aside the rubble, making space for a new wall. They cleared out the ashes of the burnt down gates. Then Aba began bringing up large stones while Penina sealed the openings between them. She was glad that she'd helped her father begin the fence back at home. Now she knew exactly what to do.

Label each word in the passage with its part of speech.

Appendix A: The 24 Books of the Tanach

The 5 Books of the Torah

1) בראשית Bereisis (Genesis)

2) שמות Shemos (Exodus)

3) ויקרא Vayikra (Leviticus)

4) במדבר Bamidbar (Numbers)

5) דברים Devarim (Deuteronomy)

The 8 Books of the Prophets (Neviim)

6) יהושע Yehoshua (Joshua)

7) שופטים Shoftim (Judges)

8) שמואל Shmuel (Samuel)

9) מלכים Melachim (Kings)

10) ישיהו Yeshayahu (Isaiah)

11) ירמיהו Yirmiyahu (Jeremiah)

12) יחזקל Yechezkel (Ezekiel)

13) תרי עשר Trei Assar (The Twelve Minor Prophets)

The 11 Books of the Writings (Kesuvim)

14) תהילים Tehillim (Psalms)

15) משלי Mishlei (Proverbs)

16) איוב Iyov (Job)

17) שיר השירים Shir HaShirim (Song of Songs)

18) רות Rus (Ruth)

19) איכה Eicha (Lamentations)

20) קהלת Koheles (Ecclesiastes)

21) אסתר Esther

22) דניאל Daniel

23) עזרא/נחמיה Ezra/Nechemia (Ezra/Nehemiah)

24) דיברי הימים Divrei Hayamim (Chronicles)

Appendix B

Required reading
Spine texts:

Option 1:
- Little Midrash Says on the Parsha (5 volume set)
- Family Midrash Says (Yehoshua, Shoftim, Shmuel I, Shmuel II, Kings I, Kings II, Daniel - 7 volumes)
- Book of Ruth, Artscroll's Children Edition
- Book of Yonah, Artscroll's Children Edition
- Artscroll's Children's Megillah
- *The Complete Story of Purim* by Nissan Mindel

Option 2:
- *A Treasury of Aggados on the Torah* by Y. Klapholtz (4 volume set)
- *A Treasury of Aggados on Nach* by Y. Klapholtz (4 volume set)
- Book of Ruth, Artscroll's Children Edition
- Book of Yonah, Artscroll's Children Edition

- Artscroll's Children's Megillah

Literature:
- *The Prisoner and Other Tales of Faith* by Rabbi Salomon Halpern
- *The Desert Diary* by Gadi Pollack
- *The Miracles of Elisha* by Sterna Citron
- *Ripples in Time* by Brocha Miller
- *The Return and Other Stories* by Yehudis Litvak
- *When We Left Yerushalayim* by Genendel Krohn

Grammar:
- *Grammar Land* by M. L. Nesbitt

Books for additional reading

Elementary:
— *Shpeter* by Rabbi Meir Uri Gottesman
— *My Last Year in Mitzrayim* by Chaim Greenbaum
— *Dovid Hamelech* by Rabbi Nachman Seltzer
— *The Secret Tunnel* by Joy Nelkin Wieder

Middle Grades/High School:

— *Dual Discovery* by Zecharia Hoffman
— *Lamp of Darkness* by Dave Mason and Mike Feuer
— *The Decree* by Rebbetzin Sarah Feldbrand
— *The Gilded Cage* by Sorale Brownstein

Recommended music
> Month 1: *I Made this World for You* by Rabbi Mordechai Dubin
> Month 2: *Let My People Go* by Rabbi Mordechai Dubin
> Month 3: *Ein Od Milvado by Yaakov Shwekey and Shlomi Shabat*
> *Month 4:* Rabbi Levi Sudri on the Book of Yehoshua
> Month 5: Harp music by Shoshanna Harrari
> Month 6: *Lakol Zman* by Uri Davidi
> Month 7: *Mama Rochel* by Yaakov Shwekey
> Month 8: Babylonian Jewish music
> Month 9: *Shoshanat Ya'akov* by Shlomo Katz
> Month 10: *Veheishiv Lev Avos* by Avraham Fried

Recommended art
    Month 1: Yoram Raanan's Biblical art
    Month 2: Ellen Miller Braun's microcalligraphy Hebrew art
    Month 3: The Mishkan
    Month 4: The Seven Trumpets of Jericho by James Tissot
    Month 5: Baruch Nachshon's Illustrated Tehillim
    Month 6: *Sacred Vessels and Vestments of the Holy Temple* exhibition at the Temple Institute
    Month 7: *The Prophet Jeremiah* by Marc Chagall
    Month 8: *Belshazzar's Feast* by Rembrandt
    Month 9: Glazed brick relief from the royal palace in Shushan (Susa)
    Month 10: *Nehemiah Views the Ruins of Jerusalem Walls* by Gustave Dore

Recommended poetry
> Month 1: Shabbat Hayom L'hashem
> Month 2: Song of the Sea in Shemos/Exodus 15:1-19
> Month 3: Song of Haazinu in Devarim 32:1-43
> *Month 4:* Song of Devorah in Shoftim (Judges) 5:1-31
> Month 5: *Tehillim* (Psalm)23
> Month 6: *Koheles* (Ecclesiastes) 3:1-8
> Month 7: *Eicha* (Lamentations 1:1-8)
> Month 8: Yechezkel (Ezekiel) 11:17-24
> Month 9: Shoshanat Yaakov
> Month 10: Malachi 3:1-6

Map list
1) Map of Ur Kasdim, Charan, and Canaan
2) Map of Canaan and Egypt
3) Map of Egypt and Sinai desert
4) Map of the Transjordan and the Land of Israel
5) Map of the Land of Israel with portions by tribe
6) Map of the Land of Israel with Jerusalem
7) Map of the Land of Israel with kingdoms of Yehuda and Yisrael
8) Map of the Land of Israel and Mesopotamia
9) Map of Mesopotamia
10) Map of the Persian Empire
11) Map of the Land of Israel and Mesopotamia

Printed in France by Amazon
Brétigny-sur-Orge, FR